ISBN 978-0-364-74751-3
PIBN 11271717

This book is a reproduction of an important historical work. Forgotten Books uses
state-of-the-art technology to digitally reconstruct the work, preserving the original format
whilst repairing imperfections present in the aged copy. In rare cases, an imperfection in
the original, such as a blemish or missing page, may be replicated in our edition. We do,
however, repair the vast majority of imperfections successfully; any imperfections that
remain are intentionally left to preserve the state of such historical works.

1 MONTH OF
FREE
READING

at
www.ForgottenBooks.com

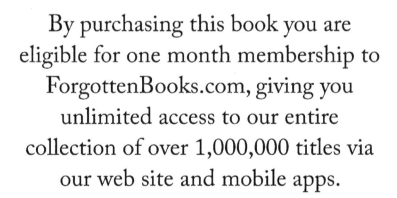

By purchasing this book you are eligible for one month membership to ForgottenBooks.com, giving you unlimited access to our entire collection of over 1,000,000 titles via our web site and mobile apps.

To claim your free month visit:

www.forgottenbooks.com/free1271717

English
Français
Deutsche
Italiano
Español
Português

www.forgottenbooks.com

Mythology Photography **Fiction**
Fishing Christianity **Art** Cooking
Essays Buddhism Freemasonry
Medicine **Biology** Music **Ancient**
Egypt Evolution Carpentry Physics
Dance Geology **Mathematics** Fitness
Shakespeare **Folklore** Yoga Marketing
Confidence Immortality Biographies
Poetry **Psychology** Witchcraft
Electronics Chemistry History **Law**
Accounting **Philosophy** Anthropology
Alchemy Drama Quantum Mechanics
Atheism Sexual Health **Ancient History**
Entrepreneurship Languages Sport
Paleontology Needlework Islam
Metaphysics Investment Archaeology
Parenting Statistics Criminology
Motivational

Historic, Archive Document

Do not assume content reflects current scientific knowledge, policies, or practices.

FALL 1927

NURSERY AND OFFICE
CRAWFORD AND PETERSON AVENUES
PHONE JUNIPER 0048
CHICAGO, ILLINOIS
and
LIBERTYVILLE, ILLINOIS
Libertyville 676J1

LEESLEY BROTHERS
NURSERIES

NURSERY AND OFFICE

CRAWFORD AND PETERSON AVENUES
Phone Juniper 0048
CHICAGO, ILLINOIS
and
LIBERTYVILLE, ILLINOIS
Libertyville 676J1

LEESLEY BROTHERS
NURSERIES

Our Chicago Nursery is located in the northwest part of the city. The Crawford Ave. car line runs within one-half mile of the Nursery. Our Libertyville Nursery is located two miles northwest of the town on Milwaukee Ave. or Route 21, which is now paved to the entrance of our Nursery.

Two branches of the Northwestern Railroad running through our grounds with a private switch, warehouse and packing sheds, the Chicago, Milwaukee and St. Paul R. R. at a short distance, all of the Express Companies near at hand offer us unsurpassed facilities for shipping stock. In addition to this we have installed three motor trucks to insure quick deliveries. For this service we shall make a charge to cover cost.

REMITTANCES

should be made by Postal or Express Money Orders, Bank Drafts on Chicago or by Registered Letters, made payable to the order of LEESLEY BROS.

PRICES

do not include packing, which will be charged for at cost. Five will be furnished at the 10 rate and 25 at the 100 rate. No charge for delivery to the express companies or railroad. Certificate of inspection furnished with each shipment.

ORNAMENTAL TREES

	Each	Per 10	Per 100
ACER dasycarpum (Silver-leaved Maple)			
1½ to 2-inch	$2.25	$20.00	
2 to 2½-inch	3.25	30.00	
2½ to 3-inch	3.75	35.00	
platanoides (Norway Maple)			
8 to 10 feet	2.00	17.50	
1¼ to 1½-inch	2.75	25.00	
3-inch	7.50		
4-inch	10.00		
wieri (Wiers C. L. Maple)			
6 to 8-feet	1.00		
AESCULUS hippocastinum (Horse Chestnut)			
3 to 3½-inch	9.00		
3½ to 4-inch	10.00		
AILANTHUS glandulosa (Tree of Heaven)			
4 to 5-feet	.60	5.00	$45.00
5 to 6-feet	.75	6.00	55.00
6 to 8-feet	.85	7.50	
8 to 10-feet	1.25	11.00	
BETULA papyrifera (Paper or Canoe Birch)			
6 to 8 feet	1.50	12.50	
8 to 10-feet	2.00	17.50	
1¼ to 1½-inch	2.50	22.50	
CATALPA bungei (Chinese)			
2-year—4-foot stems	1.50	12.50	115.00
2-year—5-foot stems	1.75	15.00	140.00
2-year—6-foot stems	2.00	17.50	165.00
3-year—5-foot stems	2.25	20.00	
3-year—6-foot stems	2.50	22.50	
speciosa (Western Catalpa)			
1¼ to 1½-inch	1.10	9.00	
1½ to 2-inch	1.75	15.00	
2 to 2½-inch	2.50	22.50	
FRAXINUS americana (American White Ash)			
1¼ to 1½-inch	1.25	11.00	100.00
1½ to 2-inch	1.75	15.00	
2 to 2½-inch	2.25	20.00	
GLEDITSIA triacanthos (Honey Locust)			
6 to 8-feet	.90	7.50	60.00
8 to 10-feet	1.00	8.50	75.00
1¼ to 1½-inch	1.50	12.50	
1½ to 1¾-inch	1.75	15.00	
1¾ to 2-inch	2.00	17.50	
GYMNOCLADUS canadensis (Kentucky Coffee Tree)			
4 to 5-feet	.75	6.00	55.00

	Each	Per 10	Per 100
JUGLANS nigra (Black Walnut)			
3 to 4-feet....................................	$0.50	$ 4.00	
POPULUS italica (Lombardy Poplar)			
6 to 8-feet....................................	.50	4.00	$35.00
8 to 10-feet....................................	.75	6.00	50.00
1¼ to 1½-inch...............................	1.00	8.50	75.00
1½ to 1¾-inch...............................	1.25	11.00	100.00
1¾ to 2 -inch...............................	1.75	16.00	150.00
2-inch	2.25	20.00	
monilifera (Carolina Poplar)			
1¼ to 1½-inch...............................	.50	4.50	40.00
1½ to 1¾-inch...............................	1.00	8.50	75.00
1¾ to 2 -inch...............................	1.25	11.00	100.00
2 to 2½-inch...............................	1.75	16.00	150.00
2½ to 3 -inch...............................	2.50	22.50	
3 to 3½-inch...............................	3.50	30.00	
PTELIA trifoliata (Hoptree)			
4 to 5-feet....................................	.60	5.00	
QUERCUS alba (White Oak)			
3 to 4-feet....................................	1.00	8.50	
palustris (Pin Oak)			
8 to 10-feet....................................	2.50		
rubra (Red Oak)			
6 to 8-feet....................................	1.75	15.00	
ROBINIA pseud acacia (Black Locust)			
2 to 3-feet (trans.)...........................	.15	1.00	8.00
hispida			
2 to 3-feet....................................	.40	3.50	
SALIX britzensis (Red Willow)			
4 to 6-feet....................................	.50	4.00	30.00
caprea (Pussy Willow)			
3 to 4-feet....................................	.35	3.00	25.00
5 to 6-feet....................................	.50	4.00	35.00
6 to 8-feet....................................	.60	5.00	
pentandra (Laurel-leaf Willow)			
4 to 5-feet....................................	.40	3.50	30.00
8 to 10-feet....................................	.75	6.00	50.00
vitellina (Russian Golden Willow)			
6 to 8-feet....................................	.60	5.00	40.00
8 to 10-feet....................................	.75	6.00	
viminalis (Basket Willow)			
6 to 8-feet....................................	1.00	7.50	60.00
SORBUS aucuparia (Mountain Ash)			
6 to 8-feet....................................	1.00		
TILIA americana (Linden or Basswood)			
1¼ to 1½-inch...............................	2.25	20.00	
1½ to 1¾-inch...............................	2.50	22.50	
1¾ to 2-inch...............................	3.00	27.50	
2 to 2½-inch...............................	3.50	32.50	
ULMUS americana (American White Elm)			
8 to 10-feet....................................	1.50	12.50	
1¼ to 1½-inch...............................	2.00	17.50	
1½ to 1¾-inch...............................	2.50	22.50	
1¾ to 2 -inch...............................	3.00	27.50	
2 to 2½-inch...............................	3.75	35.00	
2½ to 3 -inch...............................	4.25	40.00	
3 to 3½-inch...............................	6.00	55.00	
3½ to 4 -inch...............................	7.50		
4 to 4¼-inch...............................	9.00		

MORUS tatarica pendula (Tea's Weeping Mulberry)

	Each	Per 10	Per 100
2-year heads	$2.75	$25.00	

FRUITS (Bearing Size)

APPLES

Duchess	N. W. Greening
Fameuse	Talman Sweet
Grime's Golden	Wealthy
Jonathan	Pewaukee
King	Red Astrachan
McIntosh	Winesap
Yellow Transparent	Delicious
Northern Spy	

¾ and up..................................	.50	4.50	$ 40.00
1 to 1½-inch..............................	.90	8.50	80.00
1½ to 2-inch..............................	1.35	12.50	115.00
2-inch	2.50	22.50	

CRABS

Whitney	Yellow Siberian
Hyslop	Early Strawberry
Red Siberian	

¾ to 1-inch...............................	.65	5.50
1 to 1½-inch..............................	1.00	9.00
1½ to 2-inch..............................	1.50	13.50

CHERRIES

Early Richmond
Montmorency

¾ to 1-inch...............................	.75	6.50	60.00
1-inch	1.25	10.00	90.00
1½-inch	1.50	12.50	

PEARS

Kieffer	Flemish Beauty
Bartlett	Seckel
Duchess	Dwarf Duchess

¾ to 1-inch...............................	.90	7.50	65.00
1 to 1¼-inch..............................	1.10	9.00	

PLUMS

Lombard	De Soto
Prune	Abundance
Shrop Damson	Bradshaw
Burbank	

¾ to 1-inch...............................	.90	7.50	60.00
1 to 1½-inch..............................	1.35	12.50	

SMALL FRUITS

BLACKBERRIES
Snyder
Eldorado

	Each	Per 10	Per 100
Mersereau			
3-year	$0.20	$1.50	$10.00

CURRANTS
President Wilder
Fay's Prolific

Cherry			
2-year	.20	1.50	12.00
3-year	.25	2.00	15.00

GOOSEBERRIES

Downing	Champion		
Houghton	Industry		
2-year	.20	1.75	15.00

GRAPES
Concord

2-year	.20	1.75	15.00
3-year	.25	2.00	18.00

Moore's Early	Niagara		
Moore's Diamond	Agawam		
3-year	.30	2.50	22.00

RASPBERRIES
Columbia
Cumberland

Golden Queen			
2-year	.12	1.00	8.00

STRAWBERRIES
Standard varieties .... $0.75 per 100; $ 6.00 per 1,000
Everbearing .... 1.50 per 100; 12.00 per 1,000

SHRUBS

	Each	Per 10	Per 100
ALTHEA (Rose of Sharon) (in Variety)			
Bush form, 2 to 3-feet	$0.40	$3.00	$25.00
Bush form, 3 to 4-feet	.50	4.00	35.00
AMELANCHIER canadensis (Juneberry)			
2 to 3-feet	.30	2.75	25.00
ARALIA pentaphylla			
2 to 3-feet	.30	2.50	
3 to 4-feet	.40	3.00	
BERBERIS thunbergi (Japanese Barberry)			
1½ to 2-feet	.20	1.75	15.00
2 to 2½-feet	.25	2.25	20.00
2½ to 3-feet	.35	3.25	30.00

6

4 to 5-feet..................................	.40	3.00	
alternifolia			
4 to 5-feet..................................	.75	6.00	
paniculata (Gray Dogwood)			
2 to 3-feet..................................	.35	3.00	
3 to 4-feet..................................	.40	3.50	
stolonifera (Red O'sier Dogwood)			
3 to 4-feet..................................	.30	2.50	22.00
stolonifera var. aurea (Yellow Dogwood)			
2 to 3-feet..................................	.30	2.50	20.00
CORYLUS americana (Common Hazel)			
2 to 3-feet..................................	.40	3.50	
3 to 4-feet..................................	.45	4.00	
COTONEASTER acutifolia			
3 to 4-feet..................................	.50	4.00	
CRATAEGUS coccinea			
2 to 3-feet..................................	.75	6.00	
3 to 4-feet..................................	.85	7.50	60.00
4 to 5-feet..................................	1.00	8.50	75.00
crus galli			
2 to 3-feet..................................	.65	6.00	
3 to 4-feet..................................	.80	7.50	
oxyacantha (English Thorn)			
3 to 4-feet..................................	.60	5.50	50.00
4 to 5-feet..................................	.75	6.50	60.00
CYDONIA japonica (Japan Quince)			
2½ to 3-feet..................................	.40	3.50	30.00
DEUTZIA crenata			
3 to 4-feet..................................	.30	2.50	22.00
5 to 6-feet..................................	.40	3.50	
Pride of Rochester			
2½ to 3-feet..................................	.30	2.50	20.00
3 to 4-feet..................................	.35	3.00	25.00
ELEAGNUS angustifolia (Oleaster)			
3 to 4-feet..................................	.35	3.00	25.00
4 to 5-feet..................................	.40	3.50	30.00
FORSYTHIA intermedia (Golden Bell)			
2½ to 3-feet..................................	.25	2.25	20.00
3 to 4-feet..................................	.30	2.50	22.00
fortunei			
2½ to 3-feet..................................	.25	2.25	20.00
3 to 4-feet..................................	.30	2.50	22.00
HAMAMELIS virginiana (Witch Hazel)			
1 to 1½-feet..................................	.35	3.00	25.00
1½ to 2-feet..................................	.40	3.50	30.00
2 to 3-feet..................................	.45	4.00	
HYDRANGEA arborescens grandiflora (Snowball Hydrangea)			
1½ to 2-feet..................................	.40	3.50	30.00
2 to 3-feet..................................	.50	4.00	35.00
3 to 4-feet..................................	.60	5.00	
paniculata grandiflora (Bush Form) (Large Flowering Hydrangea)			
2 to 3-feet..................................	.50	4.00	35.00
3 to 4-feet..................................	.60	5.00	45.00

LIGUSTRUM amurense (Amoor River Privet)

	Each	Per 10	Per 100	Per 1,000
1½ to 2-feet	$0.15	$1.00	$ 9.00	$ 80.00
2 to 3-feet (3 to 5 canes)	.20	1.50	12.00	100.00
(5 canes and up)	.25	2.00	15.00	120.00
3 to 4-feet (Heavy)	.30	2.25	18.00	160.00
4 to 5-teet (10 canes and up) (extra heavy)	.35	2.50	20.00	.....

ibota (Chinese Privet)

	Each	Per 10	Per 100
1½ to 2-feet	.15	1.25	10.00
2 to 2½-feet	.20	1.50	12.00
2½ to 3-feet	.25	2.00	16.00
3 to 4-feet (Heavy)	.30	2.50	20.00

regelianum (Regel's Privet)

2 to 2½-feet	.30	2.75	25.00

LONICERA bella albida (White Honeysuckle)

2 to 3-feet	.25	2.00	15.00
3 to 4-feet	.30	2.50	20.00
4 to 5-feet	.40	3.50	30.00
5 to 6-feet	.50	4.00	35.00

bella chrysantha

2½ to 3-feet	.25	2.00	15.00
3 to 4-feet	.30	2.50	20.00

grandiflora (Pink Honeysuckle)

2 to 3-feet	.25	2.00	15.00
3 to 4-feet	.30	2.50	20.00
4 to 5-feet	.40	3.50	30.00

morrowi

2½ to 3-feet	.30	2.50	20.00
3 to 4-feet	.35	3.00	25.00

tatarica rosea (pink)

3 to 4-feet	.35	3.00	25.00

MALUS ioensis angustifolia (Bechtel's Double Flowering Crab)

2 to 3-feet	.60	5.00	
3 to 4-feet	.85	7.50	

ioensis (Wild Crab Apple)

2 to 3-feet	.60	5.00	
3 to 4-feet	.70	6.00	

floribunda (Japanese Crab Apple)

2 to 3-feet	.50	4.50	
3 to 4-feet	.75	6.00	55.00

MORUS alba (Russian Mulberry)

2½ to 3-feet	.15	1.25	8.00
3 to 4-feet	.20	1.75	12.00
4 to 5-feet	.25	2.25	20.00

PHILADELPHUS, coronarius (Mock Orange)

2 to 3 feet	.25	2.25	20.00
3 to 4-feet	.30	2.50	22.00
4 to 5-feet	.40	3.50	30.00

8

	Each	Per 10	Per 100
2 to 3-feet	$0.25	$ 2.00	$18.00
3 to 4-feet	.30	2.50	22.00
4 to 5-feet	.40	3.50	30.00

lemoinei

| 2 to 3-feet | .35 | 3.00 | |

nivalis

| 2 to 3-feet | .25 | 2.25 | |
| 3 to 4-feet | .30 | 2.50 | |

POTENTILLA fruticosa

| 1½ to 2-feet | .35 | 3.00 | |
| 2 to 2½-feet | .40 | 3.50 | |

PRUNUS Americana (Native Plum)

| 3 to 4-feet | .35 | 3.00 | 25.00 |
| 4 to 5-feet | .40 | 3.50 | 30.00 |

Besseyi (Bessey Cherry)

| 3 to 4-feet | .40 | 3.50 | |
| 4 to 5-feet | .50 | 4.00 | |

Othello (purple leaved Plum)

| 3 to 4-feet | .60 | 5.00 | |
| 4 to 5-feet | .75 | 6.50 | |

padus (Bird Cherry)

2 to 3-feet	.35	3.00	25.00
3 to 4-feet	.40	3.50	30.00
5 to 6-feet	.60	5.50	50.00

serotina (Black Cherry)

| 4 to 5-feet | .40 | 3.50 | 30.00 |
| 5 to 6-feet | .60 | 5.50 | |

sinensis (Pink and White) (Fl. Almond)

| 2 to 3-feet | .60 | 5.00 | |

triloba (flowering Plum)

| 2½ to 3-feet | .40 | 3.50 | |
| 3 to 4-feet | .50 | 4.00 | |

virginiana

| 5 to 6-feet | .50 | 4.50 | 40.00 |

RHAMNUS frangula

| 2 to 3-feet | .30 | 2.50 | 20.00 |
| 3 to 4-feet | .35 | 3.00 | 25.00 |

Catharticus (Buckthorn)

2 to 3-feet	.20	1.75	15.00
3 to 4-feet	.25	2.00	17.50
4 to 5-feet	.35	3.00	25.00

RHUS typhina (Staghorn Sumach)

2 to 3-feet	.25	2.00	16.00
3 to 4-feet	.30	2.50	20.00
4 to 5-feet	.35	3.00	25.00
5 to 6-feet	.45	3.50	

typhina laciniata (Cut-leaved Sumach)

| 3 to 4-feet | .35 | 3.00 | 25.00 |

RIBES Alpinum (Mountain Currant)

| 1 to 1½-feet | .35 | 2.75 | 25.00 |
| 1½ to 2-feet | .40 | 3.50 | 30.00 |

Aureum (Yellow Fl. Currant)

| 2 to 3-feet | .30 | 2.75 | 25.00 |
| 3 to 4-feet | .40 | 3.50 | |

9

ROSA blanda	Each	Per 10	Per 100
1½ to 2-feet	$0.30	$2.50	$22.00
2 to 3-feet	.35	3.00	25.00
3 to 4-feet	.40	3.50	30.00
carolina (Swamp Rose)			
1½ to 2-feet	.30	2.50	20.00
2 to 2½-feet	.35	3.00	25.00
multiflora			
3 to 4-feet	.35	3.00	25.00
rugosa (Red Japanese Rose)			
2½ to 3-feet	.35	3.00	27.50
3 to 4-feet	.45	4.00	35.00
rugosa alba (white)			
2 to 3-feet	.40	3.50	
Setigera (Prairie Rose)			
1½ to 2-feet	.25	2.00	
2 to 3-feet	.30	2.50	22.50
3 to 4-feet	.40	3.00	25.00
Wichuriana (Memorial Rose)			
2-year	.30	2.50	
ROSES, Hybrid Tea (Field Grown)			
Gruss an Teplitz	.50	4.50	40.00
ROSES, Hybrid Perpetual (Field Grown)			
Frau Karl Druschki (white)			
Magna Charta (pink, large flowering)			
Gen. Jacqueminot (bright crimson)			
Mrs. John Laing (soft pink)			
Paul Neyron (pink)			
Mme. Plantier (white)			
Harrison's Yellow (deep golden yellow)			
Ulrich Brunner (red)			
2-year	.50	4.50	40.00
ROSES, Climbing			
Excelsa (red)			
Dorothy Perkins (pink)			
Hiawatha (crimson, white eye)			
Crimson Rambler (deep crimson)			
Prairie Queen			
Flower of Fairfield (crimson, everblooming)			
American Beauty (red)			
Paul's Scarlet Runner (scarlet)			
Tousandschon (pink and white)			
2-year	.40	3.50	25.00
3-year	.50	4.00	35.00
SAMBUCUS aureus (Golden Elder)			
2 to 3-feet	.35	3.00	25.00
3 to 4-feet	.40	3.50	
Canadensis (Common Elder)			
3 to 4-feet	.35	2.50	22.00
4 to 5-feet	.40	3.50	30.00
5 to 6-feet	.50	4.50	40.00
Laciniata (C. L. Elder)			
3 to 4-feet	.35	3.00	25.00
4 to 5-feet	.40	3.50	30.00
SPIRÆA Anthony Waterer			
1½ to 2-feet	.35	3.00	25.00
arguta (white)			
1½ to 2-feet	.25	2.25	20.00
2 to 3-feet	.40	3.50	30.00
Bethlehemensis (pink)			
2½ to 3-feet	.25	2.00	18.00
3 to 4-feet	.30	2.50	20.00
4 to 5-feet	.35	3.00	25.00

SPIRÆA (Continued)

Billardi	Each	Per 10	Per 100
2½ to 3-feet	.25	2.25	20.00
3 to 4-feet	.30	2.50	22.00
froebeli (Dwarf Pink)			
1½ to 2-feet	.25	2.00	18.00
2 to 2½-feet	.30	2.50	22.00
3-feet (Heavy)	.40	3.50	
opulifolia (Ninebark)			
2½ to 3-feet	.25	2.00	15.00
3 to 4-feet	.30	2.50	20.00
4 to 5-feet	.35	3.00	25.00
opulifolia var. aurea (Golden Spirea)			
2 to 3-feet	.30	2.50	
3 to 4-feet	.35	3.00	
van houttei (Bridal Wreath)			
2½ to 3-feet	.25	2.00	15.00
3 to 4-feet	.30	2.50	20.00
4 to 5-feet (Heavy)	.35	3.00	25.00
Thunbergi			
2 to 2½-feet	.35	3.00	25.00

SYMPHORICARPOS racemosus (Snowberry)

	Each	Per 10	Per 100
1½ to 2-feet	.20	1.50	12.00
2 to 3-feet:	.25	2.00	16.00
3 to 4-feet	.35	3.00	25.00
vulgaris (Indian Currant)			
1½ to 2-feet	.20	1.50	12.00
2 to 3-feet	.25	2.00	15.00

SYRINGA alba (White Lilac)

	Each	Per 10	Per 100
2 to 3-feet	.40	3.50	30.00
3 to 4-feet	.50	4.50	

French Lilacs (named varieties)
Charles Tenth   Mme. Lemoinei
Ludwig Spaeth   Pres. Grevy

	Each	Per 10	Per 100
1 to 1½-feet	.40	3.50	
1½ to 2-feet	.50	4.50	
Japonica			
4 to 5-feet	.85	7.50	
rothomagensis (Persian Lilac)			
2½ to 3-feet	.45	4.00	35.00
3 to 4-feet	.50	4.50	40.00
vulgaris (Common Purple Lilac)			
2 to 3-feet	.35	3.00	25.00
3 to 4-feet	.40	3.50	30.00

TAMARIX Amurense (Amoor River Tamarix)

	Each	Per 10	Per 100
2 to 3-feet	.25	2.00	18.00
3 to 4-feet	.30	2.50	20.00
4 to 5-feet	.40	3.50	30.00
hispida aestivalis			
2 to 3-feet	.35	2.50	
3 to 4-feet	.40	3.00	

VIBURNUM dentatum (Arrow-wood)

	Each	Per 10	Per 100
2 to 3-feet	.35	3.00	25.00
3 to 4-feet	.40	3.75	35.00
4 to 5-feet	.50	4.00	
lantana (English Wayfaring Tree)			
2 to 3-feet	.50	4.50	
lentago (Sheepberry)			
2 to 3-feet	.40	3.50	
3 to 4-feet	.50	4.50	

VIBURNUM (Continued)

	Each	Per 10	Per 100
opulus (H. B. Cranberry) (Pembina)			
1½ to 2-feet	$0.35	$3.00	$27.50
2 to 3-feet	.45	4.00	37.50
1½ to 2-feet	.35	3.00	
opulus nanum (Dwarf H. B. Cranberry)			
12 to 15-inch	.35	3.00	
opulus sterilis (Snowball)			
2 to 3-feet	.50	4.50	
WEIGELA Eva Rathke (red)			
2 to 3-feet	.40	3.50	
3 to 4-feet	.50		
2 to 3-feet	.30	2.50	20.00
rosea (pink)			
2 to 3-feet	.30	2.50	20.00
3 to 4-feet	.35	3.00	25.00
XANTHOXYLUM americanum (Prickly Ash)			
5 to 6-feet	.50	4.00	

CLIMBING VINES

	Each	Per 10	Per 100
AMPELOPSIS engelmanni (Englemann's Ivy)			
2-year	.25	2.00	15.00
3-year	.30	2.50	20.00
quinquefolia (Virginia Creeper)			
3-year	.25	2.25	20.00
veitchi (Boston Ivy)			
2-year	.40	3.50	
ARISTOLOCHIA sipho (grafted) (Dutchman's Pipe)			
2-year	.60	5.00	
CELASTRUS orbiculatus (Oriental Bittersweet)			
2-year	.25	2.00	17.50
3-year	.30	2.50	20.00
Scandens (American Bittersweet)			
2-year	.25	2.00	17.50
3-year	.30	2.50	20.00
CLEMATIS Jackmanni (purple)			
2-year	.50	4.00	
henryi			
2-year	.50	4.00	
paniculata (white)			
2-year	.25	2.00	15.00
LONICERA halleana (Hall's Honeysuckle)			
2-year	.25	2.00	15.00
sempervirens (Scarlet Trumpet Honeysuckle)			
2-year	.25	2.00	15.00
3-year	.30	2.50	
LYCIUM sinensis (Matrimony Vine)			
3-year	.25	2.25	20.00
VITIS aestivalis (Wild Grape)			
2-year	.30	2.50	**20.00**
3-year	.35	3.00	25.00
WISTARIA sinensis (Chinese Blue Wistaria)			
3-year	.40	3.50	

RHUBARB

	Each	Per 10	Per 100
LINNEAUS			
3-year	.25	1.75	15.00

ASPARAGUS

	Per 100	Per 1000
Conovers and Palmetto		
2-year	$2.00	$12.00

12

EVERGREEN

	Each	Per 10	Per 100
ABIES concolor			
3-feet	$6.50	$60.00	
JUNIPERUS communis (Var. Canadensis)			
1 to 1½-foot spread	1.75	15.00	
1½ to 2-foot spread	2.25	20.00	
2 to 2½-foot spread	3.00	27.50	
Pfitzeriana			
12 to 15-inch spread	1.50	12.50	
15 to 18-inch spread	1.75	15.00	
1½ to 2-foot spread	2.50	22.50	
2 to 2½-foot spread	3.50	30.00	
Sabina			
1 to 1½-feet	2.75	25.00	
1½ to 2-feet	3.50	32.50	
Virginiana (Red Cedar)			
3 to 4-feet	3.50	32.50	
4 to 5-feet	4.75	45.00	
Virginiana glauca			
3 to 4-feet	6.00		
PICEA alba (White Spruce)			
1-foot	.75	6.00	
1½ to 2-feet	1.75	15.00	
2 to 2½-feet	2.25	20.00	
2½ to 3-feet	2.75	25.00	
3 to 4-feet	3.50	32.50	
4 to 5-feet	5.00	45.00	
Canadensis (Black Hill Spruce)			
1½-feet	1.75	15.00	
2 to 2½-feet	2.25	20.00	
3-feet	3.50	32.50	
Excelsa (Norway Spruce)			
1½ to 2-feet	1.00	8.00	
2 to 2½-feet	1.75	15.00	
2½ to 3-feet	2.25	20.00	
3 to 4-feet	2.50	22.50	
4 to 5-feet	3.25	30.00	
6 to 7-feet	5.75	55.00	
Pungens (Colorado Green Spruce)			
1 to 1½-feet	1.75	15.00	
1½ to 2-feet	2.25	20.00	
2 to 2½-feet	2.75	25.00	
2½ to 3-feet	3.75	35.00	
Pungens glauca (Colorado Blue Spruce)			
1 to 1½-feet	3.75	35.00	
1½ to 2-feet	4.75	45.00	
2 to 2½-feet	6.50	60.00	
2½ to 3-feet	8.00	75.00	
PINUS strobus (White Pine)			
3 to 4-feet	3.25	30.00	
4 to 5-feet	4.75	45.00	
5 to 6-feet	5.75	50.00	
6 to 7-feet	6.75	65.00	
Austriaca (Austrian Pine)			
2½ to 3-feet	3.75	35.00	
3 to 4-feet	4.75	45.00	
Mughus (Mugho Pine)			
1 to 1½-feet	2.75	25.00	
1½ to 2-feet	3.75	35.00	

Ponderosa	Each	Per 10	Per 100
4 to 5-feet	4.75	45.00	
Sylvestris (Scotch Pine)			
2 to 3-feet	2.50	22.50	
PSEUDOTSUGA douglasi (Douglas Fir)			
2½ to 3-feet	3.25	30.00	
3 to 4-feet	4.25	40.00	
THUYA occidentialis (Arbor Vitae)			
1 to 1½-feet	.75	6.00	
1½ to 2-feet	1.00	8.50	
2 to 3-feet	1.75	15.00	
3 to 4-feet	2.75	25.00	
globosa			
1 to 1½-feet	2.00	15.00	
1½ to 2-feet	2.50	22.50	

HARDY HERBACEOUS PLANTS

	Each	Per 10	Per 100
ACHILLEA Ptarmica (The Pearl)	$0.15	$ 1.25	$ 10.00
AQUILEGIA coerulea (Columbine)	.15	1.25	10.00
ALYSSUM Saxatile	.15	1.25	10.00
ANTHEMIS Kelwayi (Golden Marguerite)	.15	1.25	10.00
tinctoria (Yellow)	.15	1.25	10.00
ASTER Tataricus (Purple Aster)	.15	1.25	10.00
BELLIS Perennis	.15	1.25	10.00
BOLTONIA asteroides (White)	.20	1.50	12.00
CHRYSANTHEMUM Maximum (Shasta Daisy)	.15	1.25	10.00
King Edward III	.15	1.25	10.00
Hardy in variety	.20	1.75	15.00
CONVALLARIA Majalis (Lily of the Valley)	.15	1.25	10.00
COREOPSIS Grandiflora	.15	1.25	10.00
lanceolata	.15	1.25	10.00
DELPHINUM Belladonna (Larkspur) Light Blue	.20	1.50	12.00
formosum	.15	1.25	10.00
Gold Medal Hybrid (Larkspur) Dark Blue	.20	1.50	12.00
DIANTHUS plumarius (Hardy pinks)	.15	1.25	10.00
astro-sanguinia	.15	1.25	10.00
Barbatus	.15	1.25	10.00
DICENTRA spectabilis (Bleeding Heart)			
Clumps	.40	3.50	30.00
DIGITALIS monstrosa (Fox Glove)	.20	1.50	12.00
FUNKIA subcordata (Day Lily)	.20	1.50	12.00
GAILLARDIA grandiflora	.15	1.25	10.00
HELIOPSIS Pitcheriana	.15	1.25	10.00
HEMEROCALLIS (Lemon Lily)	.20	1.75	15.00
HIBISCUS (Crimson Eye)	.15	1.25	10.00
HOLLYHOCKS in variety	.15	1.25	10.00
IRIS German in variety	.20	1.75	15.00

Mme. Chereau	Oriole
Leopold	L'Africana
Chas. Dickens	Hayden
Hector	Canary Bird
Dalmatica	

	Each	Per 10	Per 100
pumila	.20	1.75	15.00
sibirica	.20	1.75	15.00
LINUM perenne (Flax)	.15	1.25	10.00

14

	Each	Per 10	Per 100
LYCHNIS chalceodoinca	$0.15	$1.25	$10.00
LYTHRUM roseum	.15	1.25	10.00
PACHYSANDRA terminalis	.25	2.00	16.00
PAPAVER Nudicaule	.15	1.25	10.00

PEONIES (in variety)
Festiva
Louis Van Houtte (dark crimson)
Nobilissima (deep pink)
Couronne d'Or (white, red center)
Festiva Maxima (large white)
Edulis superba (soft pink, early)
Fragrans (red)
Louis Van Houtte (dark crimson)
Duchess de Nemours (sulphur white, late)
Duke of Wellington (sulphur white, late)

	Each	Per 10	Per 100
2 to 3-eyes	.35	3.00	25.00
4 to 5-eyes	.50	4.00	35.00
5 to 7-eyes	.60	5.00	45.00

Felix Crousse (brilliant red)
Mons. Jules Elie (pale lilac rose)

	Each	Per 10	Per 100
5 to 7-eyes	.75	6.00	55.00
PHYSOSTEGIA Virginica	.15	1.25	10.00
PLATYCODON grandiflora (Chinese bell flower)	.15	1.25	10.00
Japonica	.15	1.25	10.00
Mariese (Blue)	.15	1.25	10.00
PHLOX in variety	.25	2.00	15.00

Mrs. Charles Dorr (lavender)
Bridesmaid (white with crimson center)
Eclaireur (bright rose)
R. P. Struther (cherry red)
Mrs. Jenkins (large white, early bloomer)
Thor (salmon pink, red eye)
La Vague (lavender pink)
Baron Von Dedim (brilliant red, salmon shadings)
Pantheon (rose pink)
Rynstrom (rose pink)

	Each	Per 10	Per 100
creeping (pink and white)	.15	1.25	16.00

PYRETHRUM Hybridum

	Each	Per 10	Per 100
roseum double	.15	1.25	10.00
Uliginosum	.15	1.25	10.06
SEDUM spectabilia (Stone crop)	.15	1.25	10.00

YUCCA

	Each	Per 10	Per 100
2-year	.20	1.50	10.00
3-year	.25	1.75	15.00
GRASSES in var.	.15	1.20	

BOXING and PACKING CHARGES

30x30x14-feet	$5.50	24x24x10-feet	$3.50
30x30x12-feet	5.00	20x20x10-feet	3.00
30x30x10-feet	4.50	18x18x10-feet	2.75
24x30x12-feet	4.50	16x16x10-feet	2.50
24x30x10-feet	4.00	14x14x10-feet	2.25
24x24x12-feet	4.00	12x12x10-feet	1.75

15

CPSIA information can be obtained
at www.ICGtesting.com
Printed in the USA
LVHW040725271218
601879LV00012B/135/P